The comforts of home.

The latest gramophone was the handmade 'Expert' of 1931; the latest radio (also 1931) was the deco styled Ecko Consolette at 24 guineas, which had a bakelite case and, for the first time, a dial which named the different radio stations such as Radio Normandie and Budapest. This radio came in a choice of "three delightful shades" — dark jade, mahogany and walnut. The public wanted more colour in their homes, especially in the kitchen where the housewife now spent more of her time. Cookers could be purchased with a variety of coloured trimmings, the telephone and the Anglepoise lamp came in four colours, and Lloyd Loom furniture was obtainable in any colour. The HMV television set of 1938 has a six inch screen.

2

INTRODUCTION

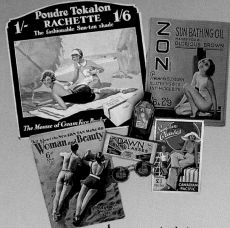

A suntan had become the fashionable accessory. The Hollywood couple Ben Lyon and Bebe Daniels sunbathe on the cover of Woman and Beauty (1932).

Whereas the 1920s had been an era of recovery from the Great War – a period of comparative tranquility – the 1930s was a time of increasing political tension, with unemployment approaching three million by 1932. For many there was a prevailing feeling of gloom, not helped by Aldous Huxley's depressing vision of the future in his book 'Brave New World' or George Orwell's unsparing picture of unemployment in 'The Road to Wigan Pier'.

Nevertheless, amongst ordinary people there was great optimism for the future. Homes and cars were more affordable than ever before, the radio had matured as a varied source of entertainment, the telephone service 'instantly' connected two million subscribers in 1931 – the year in which the London telephone directory split into two volumes – electric appliances and gadgets helped the shortfall in domestic servants, and the cinema provided an escape into a glamorous fantasy life.

Political extremes:
The right wing Blackshirt newssheet was launched in February 1933; the left wing International Brigade banded together to fight Franco in Spain's Civil War (1936-1939). For the first time the world could see the damage inflicted by air raids.

The era had its heroes and villains. Amy Johnson captured the public imagination with her aviation exploits (songs, records and dolls celebrated her achievements); Shirley Temple was the child star and darling of the silver screen (with her 'own' breakfast cereal); but Mrs Wallace Simpson was simply the woman "who pinched our king".

The 1930s was a time of price stability: the Radio Times cost 2d throughout the decade, a Mars bar 2d and – the cheap way of buying a book – a Penguin 6d (first published in 1935). A cultural shock for many, the speed of change was offset by nostalgia for the good old days: ladies in crinoline dresses appeared on Christmas cards, and thatched cottages on chocolate boxes. The design for the Quality Street box captured this nostalgic mood when launched in 1935. Indeed there was a great desire for the ideal home of yesteryear, where the tranquility of the countryside gave a sense of peace – only to be shattered by the outbreak of the Second World War.

Labour saving in the kitchen. Pyrex arrives from the USA, the Aga cooker from Sweden.

Many speed records were broken during the 1930s. The great liners vied with each other to gain the 'Blue Riband' Atlantic crossing record – a battle mainly between the French Normandie and Britain's Queen Mary. Malcolm Campbell continually broke land and water speed records. Racing cars sped round the Brooklands circuit; the Singer Ten domestic car (above centre) gained four motoring records in 1931, so everyone thought they were racers. Children had their record books and their models, like Britain's miniatures of Blue Bird (1935) and the Railton New Wonder Car driven by John Cobb at over 350 mph in 1938.

New magazines: Woman's Own in 1932 (updated in 1937 with more pages and colour), Woman in 1937 and Picture Post in 1938.

The British coastline was dotted with about 100 holiday camps by 1939, including Butlins at Skegness (1937) and Clacton (1938).

Cocktails were now available ready-mixed and savoury biscuits like Twiglets (1932) and Cheeselets joined the scene. Greater awareness of vitamins promoted brands like Bemax (1928) and the sale of 'Sunshine' in margarine. Sliced bread was an early convenience food; instant coffee arrived with Bantam in 1932 and Nescafé in 1939. Beer in a can was more of a novelty.

The fear of war centred on air raids and gas. By 1937 plans were well advanced for air raid precautions (ARP). Even cigarette cards explained ARP in 1938.

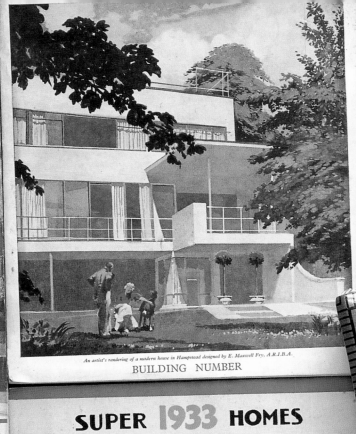

An artist's rendering of a modern house in Hampstead designed by E. Maxwell Fry, A.R.I.B.A.

BUILDING NUMBER

APRIL 1933   A MODERN HOUSE AT NEWBURY *(Plans and Particulars in This Issue)*   ONE SHILLING

THE COMPLETE GUIDE TO HOME MAKING

HOME OWNER'S HANDBOOK

2/6

HOW TO PLAN, EQUIP, SAVE MONEY ON YOU... TELLS YOU WHERE TO BUY AN...

SUPER 1933 HOMES

9/6 WEEKLY

BARNEHURST PARK ESTATE BARNEHURST, KENT

Estate Office: Station Approach, Barnehurst, Kent.
Telephone: Bexleyheath 406.

£395 FREEHOLD

NEW IDEAL HOMESTEADS...
...TAIN'S BIGGEST...

How to paint

with ROBBIALAC

1/-

BUY YOUR HOUSE

Through the
HEARTS OF OAK
BENEFIT SOCIETY

HOW CAN I BUY MY HOUSE ?

LOANS for HOMES

HALIFAX BUILDING SOCIETY

A housing boom in the early 1930s gave many people the opportunity to buy their own home. Lowering the 25% deposit to five or ten per cent from 1930 enabled a £500 house to be paid off at 13/- weekly over 22 years with a £50 down payment. Many workers earned £200 a year, so this was quite affordable.

Art deco and modernistic architecture with flat roofs appealed to some, but for many the "ideal home" was a half-timbered mock Tudor house or thatched cottage, reminiscent of old world England, with gardens full of hollyhocks, sweet peas and Canterbury bells.

DAILY MAIL IDEAL HOME EXHIBITION OLYMPIA MARCH 24 - APRIL 17 1930

DAILY MAIL IDEAL HOME EXHIBITION APRIL 3-28 OLYMPIA

WATES

THE QUALITY BUILDERS

Visit House No 6 IN THE HOUSING SECTION
Freehold Houses from
16/10 WEEKLY Including All Rates
20 Districts in South London

GUARANTEED HOUSE...

Wates Head Office: ... LONDON ROAD, NORBURY, S.W.16

4

The DELUXE MAINAMEL Cooker in GREEN and CREAM Finish

GAS COOKERS
1934

Automatic Cooking

The SOLENT
TABLE MANGLE

An improved
Self-Lifting
Machine

Talk it over with your husband

MADE BY
Ewbank

THE SILENT
SILOVAC

The
VAC

Popul

MODEL

**VACUUM
CLEANER**

£6.12.6

COMPLETE
WITH ALL
ACCESSORIES

ALL BRITISH

ELECTRICITY
DOES IT BEST OF ALL

Electric Cooking

HINTS for the MODERN HOUSEWIFE

**INTERESTING
DISHES**
prepared with...
Batchelor's Peas
IN TINS READY COOKED
AND IN PACKETS
FOR STEERING

Described
by a
FAMOUS CHEF

with notes on the use of herbs.

Nearly half a million users—

and not ONE
has spent a penny
for SERVICE
or REPA

**AUTOMATIC ELECTRIC
REFRIGERATOR**

In a B.T.H. Refrigerator food can be kept safe
during the hottest of weather.

DIRT
CANNOT ESCAPE
Vac-tric
VACUUM CLEANER

The "CONA" Coffee Machine

The
NEW WORLD
Gas Cooker
in Rado Porcelain Mottled
Enamel Finish

the new
RADIATION
RECIPE
BOOK

Bright Hints For Bright Homes

FOR EVERY
MODERN HOUSEWIFE

Use SOLAR

and BE SURE of
HOT WATER
in the morning

PIONEER

WRINGER, MANGLE and
TABLE COMBINED,
DIRECT FROM THE
MANUFACTURERS
W. J. HARRIS & Co., Ltd.
PECKHAM, LONDON.
S.E.

For the growing band of housewives with no domestic help, a range of electric appliances was the saviour of the day. The vacuum cleaner, hair drier, refrigerator, toaster, electric fire, water heater, washing machine and cooker (now electric as well as gas), all were part of the modern home along with the latest in electric lighting. The National Grid was set up in 1934 to unify the existing system. The Ewbank ad suggests, "talk it over with your husband"

With health and fitness on their minds, the figure-conscious bought crispbread, such as Ryvita and Vita-Wheat, while dietary brands produced by Energen were also much in vogue for their lack of sugar content. Granorita was a digestive biscuit, starch-reduced for 'diabetics, obesity, indigestion'. Breakfast cereals grew in demand during the 1930s. Also seen as healthy, dietary foods, they were easy to serve and did

away with the need for a cooked breakfast. The latest wheat cereal was Weetabix, which came out in 1932.
Other new products were Rover biscuits (1930), the cooking fats Trex (1931) and Spry (1936), Bourn-vita (1933),
ready-made Robinson's Lemon Barley Water in a bottle (1935), Brooke Bond Digestive tea and Dividend tea in the
mid 1930s, and Nescafé instant coffee (1939). Lucozade first appeared in 1929 being developed nationally during the 1930s.

A great time for sweet-lovers, when
confectionery firms experimented with a
variety of tastes and mixtures. Each new launch
was a notable event. Fry's Crunchies had already arrived in 1929. Terry's
created their Chocolate Orange and All Gold chocolate assortment in 1932.
Black Magic (1933) proved popular in an art deco style box; and Rowntree's
Dairy Box was added to the range in 1936. Quality Street was also launched
in 1936, and Cadbury's Roses two years later.
Mars bars were produced in Britain from 1932, followed by Milky Way (1935) and
Maltesers (1936). Other chocolate bars came in quick succession: Cadbury's Whole
Nut (1933), Aero (1935) and Chocolate Crisp (1935), renamed two years later as
Kit Kat. The sensation of 1937 was white chocolate, in the form of Nestlé's Milky
Bar (see back cover), and in the same year Smarties and Rolo appeared.

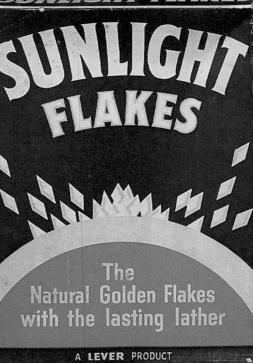

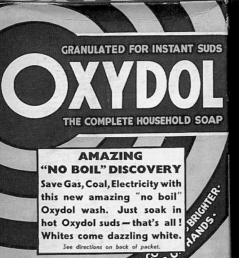

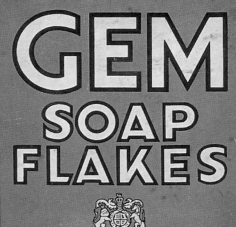

The retinue of staff who cleaned and polished and washed clothes had mostly disappeared, and the housewife was left to fend for herself. To compensate, household products continually improved in performance and effectiveness. From the USA, Brillo arrived in the late 1920s, and in 1930 Oxydol had also come over to compete with Persil, another detergent-based soap powder. Later Oxydol announced on its pack a 'No Boil' discovery. A more advanced detergent was Dreft, launched in

November 1937. It was advertised to be used for washing 'pretties' as the box illustrates: 'Only with Dreft can you avoid dulling soap scum'. Competition amongst the soap powders was intense. Large economy packs began to appear, like that for Sunlight Flakes (launched in 1938). In the mid 1930s Gracie Field's performed on the Fairy Soap programme, which was broadcast by Radio Luxembourg and Radio Normandie. Ever concious of 'dirt', housewives were happy to have antiseptics like Dettol (1932) and TCP.

13

Purpose-built bathrooms were more common in the 1930s, and more attention was given to hygiene. Bath cubes and bath salts were a cheap luxury. The price of toilet soap was drastically reduced in the early '30s, and thus everyone could afford a 3d bar of Lifebuoy (introduced 1933), Lux (1928) or Palmolive (1913). Slicked down hair for gentlemen was all the rage, with Brylcreem (1928) the most popular unguent. Cosmetics like lipstick were making their way onto every dressing table, so that even housemaids could imitate stars like Marlene Dietrich or Greta Garbo.

Having prepared the evening meal and cleaned the house, even the most dedicated housewife could allow herself to leaf through a magazine. A wide range catered for every taste: keeping up with fashion, reading the latest gossip, or enjoying a romantic story. Significantly, many magazine titles of the time included the word 'Modern'. New titles included Woman's Own, Woman, Illustrated, Picture Post and, for men, in December 1935 Men Only. The holiday number of Woman's Fair in July 1936 shows the latest in sunbathing outfits, while the mother on the cover of Woman's Pictorial (1935) checks her copy of Child Psychology for help.

TWOPENCE

...oman

...ONAL HOME WEEKLY

WELCOME ON THE MAT IS NOT ENOUGH!

WOMAN'S
2d
OWN
AND
WOMAN'S LIFE

Modern Wonder
No 1

Nº 1 OF THE NEWEST SIXPENNY

Miss-Modern
OCTOBER
6d

The Story of Our Little Princesses BEGINS INSIDE!

Wife and Home
6d

Free FROCK PATTERN Inside
HOME NOTES

KNIT JEAN HARLOW'S JUMPER
MODERN
WEEKLY
2d

Wonderful FREE GIFT Number
MODERN HOME

A String of Parisian Pearls - FREE
Inside
Modern Marriage
Nº1
6d
APRIL
1931

Prizes for "Snapshot" Stories
HOME CHAT
2

...EEN
NEWSPAPER

A Lovely FREE GIFT Inside
MODERN WOMAN
OCTOBER
6d

BRITANNIA and EVE
AUGUST
1935
1/-

No1 OF THE NEW MAGAZINE FOR...
men only
1/- NET
DECEMBER
A. P. HERBERT : BERNARD DARWIN
A. G. STREET : REGINALD ARKELL
GEOFFREY GILBEY : ETC

ROSITA FORBES writes a SPECIAL ARTICLE—INSIDE
WOMAN'S PICTORIAL
Vol. 30. No. 757. JULY 13th, 1935.
3d
Every Monday.

THE
AUGUST
HAPPY
7d
MAG.

Out of Harness!

THIS FROCK PATTERN for 6d
WOMAN'S FRIEND
No. 570. JANUARY 26, 1935.
2d

...ION :: MOTHERCRAFT :: BEAUTY :: FIC...

17

SIXPENNY SERIES No...

TENNIS WEAR

6d

Christmas FASHIONS · FICTION
BEAUTY · NEEDLEWORK

Weldon's GOOD TASTE

AND ILLUSTRATED DRESSMAKER

No. 670

DECEMBER 1935

4½d

This PATTERN FREE inside

So Easy-to-Knit!
SEE PAGE 31

This PATTERN FREE inside

This PATTERN FREE inside

This PATTERN FREE inside

New Style
JUMPER & SHOR...
worn by
...HILLIAR...
...F LON...

ALL SIZES SEE PAGE

No. 654

32 PAGE...

WELDON'S LADIES' JOURNA...
Portfolio of Fashions

OVER
90
FASHION
DESIGNS

ALL these PATTER...
FREE INSIDE

Weldon's ...ALOGUE of FASHIONS

6d

Special Offer
Pattern of this NEW TWO PIECE (DRESS a... 6...
SEE P...

...oth these Patterns inside

OVER
400
MODELS

ROMA'S FASHIONS

6d
JULY
1935

FREE
INSIDE these
2 DRESS
PATTERNS

Mabs FASHIONS

AUGUST, 1936

6d

All
these
Patterns
Inside

KNITTING INSTRUCTIONS FOR

BARGAIN PATTERN FOR ONE PIECE FULL LENGTH COAT
SEE INSIDE

SPRING & SUMMER 1936

Style 9071
Style 9093

EVANS & OWEN
BATH
LTD

J. Roussel Paris

Slimming was much in vogue; it was necessary, too, if women were to conform to the long, slender fashion line of the 1930s. However, a good foundation garment could mould the figure to the right shape. Hats ranged from giant sun hats to petite appendages perched on one side of the head. The modish fashion accessory was a tennis raquet.

Price :
...of varied ...lace
7

FREE -- ALL these Patterns

"STAR" VALUE SUITS

S.B. and D.B. STYLES

25/- EACH

A CHOICE OF THREE PATTERNS

LEACH'S BOYS' KNITTED SUITS

TWO-FOUR YEARS

6D

PRACTICAL DESIGNS WITH SIMPLE DIRECTIONS

LEACH'S SIXPENNY KNITTING & HANDCRAFT SERIES No. 162

WELDON'S BAZAAR OF CHILDREN'S FASHIONS

JANUARY 4D 1935

FREE *these* 6 PATTERNS *inside*

60 Designs · Free Transfer · Happier Babies · Cookery &c

TARANTULLE

FOR WHITE & COLOURED LINGERIE

16 page Gift Book of WOOLLIES Inside

WELDON'S BAZAAR OF CHILDREN'S FASHIONS

4D GIFT No

Made for 3/8 1 to 2 yrs.

Make this for 9/- 15 to 16 yrs.

Making costs 1/9 3 to 4 yrs.

Cost of Making 1/9 3 to 4 yrs.

FREE *these* 4 New PATTERNS Gift Book

Woollies for Baby

DRESS DISTINGUISHED BURTON DRESS

GUINEA FLANNEL SUIT 55/-

4 GUINEA PROTECTOR RAINCOAT for 35/-

TODDLERS' OUTFITS

Leach's CHILDREN'S FASHIONS No. 234

4½D

PATTERN OF BOY'S OR GIRL'S COAT AND HAT 49 WITH COUPON (1-6 YRS)

These Patterns FREE Inside

WELDON'S BAZAAR OF CHILDREN'S FASHIONS

All these Patterns FREE inside

AUGUST 4D 1934

• 60 DESIGNS
• HAPPIER BABIES
• COMPLETE STORY
• ARTICLES
• COOKERY

Modern technology meant that even the working man could afford a made-to-measure suit — a '5 guinea suit' for 55/-. Leading this revolution were Burtons, 'the tailor of taste', who claimed to be making 'tailoring history'. Men's clothes continued to become cheaper through the decade. Children's clothes, however, were generally still being made at home; the emphasis was on 'practical designs', from patterns with simple directions.

21

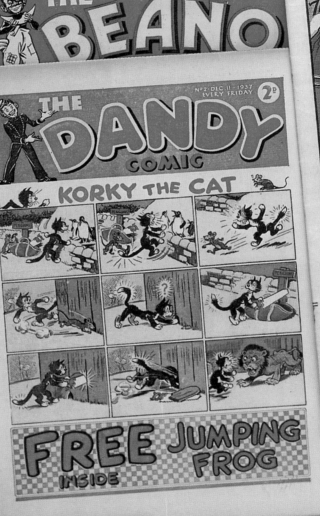

A wide variety of comics were available to children in the 1930s, although most were aimed at boys. Established titles, such as Comic Cuts, usually uncoloured, were priced at 1d while more recent arrivals, with more colour and more pages, cost 2d. Newcomers included Mickey Mouse Weekly (1936), The Dandy (1937) and The Beano (1938). Cowboys were still a favourite theme; The Ranger first appeared in 1931 and Wild West Weekly in 1938. Free gifts were part of the attraction. The Gem offered 'a working model aero-car' over three issues, while a wonderful wristlet watch was given away inside copies of the Playbox. The Ovaltineys were founded in 1935, and their own comic was inserted in existing comics, such as here, in the Rocket.

The MODERN BOY

JOLLY JACKS WEEKLY
JUNIOR SECTION—SUNDAY DISPATCH

CASH PRIZES !!! BIG NEW THRILLER
OKAY COMICS

1D. Bar of Sharp's Kreemy Toffee!
Bullseye
HITS THE MARK EVERY TIME
Every Friday 2D
Week ending January 24th, 1931. TWOPENCE.

THE DAILY MAIL, WEDNESDAY, SEPTEMBER 6, 1933.—No.
BOYS AND GIRLS
Your Own Picture Paper
Daily Mail
1933

CALLING ALL BOYS & GIRLS Nº1 OF YOUR NEW PAPER FREE GIFTS INSIDE
HAPPY DAYS 2D
No. 1 AT CHIMPO'S CIRCUS October 8, 1938 EVERY MONDAY
Tell Chimpo the circus is waiting! / I'll come when I've finished! / Chimpo is in his bath! / Fetch him here at once!

EVENINGS !
THRILLS ! See Page Three.
T 2D

Presented by the CHIEF OVAL
OVALTINEY'S OWN COMIC
Vol. 4

COMIC CUTS 1 SHORT CUTS TO LONG LAUGHS !
Comic Cuts 1
THE KING OF COMICS

RIES OF SOLO SOLOMON
Price TWOPENCE
NTURE
THIN !
2D

OVALTINEY COMIC WITHIN
ROCKET 1
Every Monday

BOYS BROADCAST · NEW STORIES EVERY WEEK
BOYS BROADCAST

TARGET 1D
Every Monday
MORE HALF-CROWNS OFFERED !
TARGET 1
EVERY MONDAY
July 6th, 19

The SPARKLER, EVERY MONDAY, 2d. BEGIN THIS STORY TO-DAY. HAL OF THE FOREST. WOODLAND MYSTERY, ROMANCE AND ADVENTURE
THE SPARKLER 2D

LS FOR YOU INSIDE, BOYS
Vol 1. No. 4 MARCH 22 1930 EVERY MONDAY 2D
ARTLER

KY-HIGH COWBOY! GREAT WAR-FLYING STORY INSIDE
BUZZER

BRIGHT THURSDAY THE SUNNIEST & THE FUNNIEST
MERRY AND BRIGHT 1D

WONDERFUL Coloured Pictures Free INSIDE!
The TRIUMPH

FREE GIFTS TO PLEASE EVERY READER ! IMPORTANT NEWS INSIDE.
THE WIZARD
Nº 723 FEB

2D THE SUNBEAM 2D
GRAND CHRISTMAS NUMBER
HAVE A MERRY CHRISTMAS.

d FREE GIFT Number
GEM 2D

FREE INSIDE—WHIZZ-BANG ARCHIE ANTI-AIRCRAFT GUN
THE SKIPPER
Nº 418 — SEPT. 3RD 1938 — PRICE 2D

WILD WEST WEEKLY
2D EVERY THURSDAY

onderful FREE GIFT!
PIONEER AERO-CAR
This Grand WORKING MODEL AERO-CAR for Every Reader
GIVEN FREE WITH THIS ISSUE

THE PAPER WITH FAMOUS FUN AND THRILL STORIES
THE HOTSPUR
Nº 320 OCT. 14TH 1939 – EVERY FRIDAY – 2D

MICKEY MOUSE WEEKLY 2D
Vol. 1. No. 1. February 8th, 1936
EVERY FRIDAY 2D

HORNBY-DUBLO TRAIN

THE PERFECT MINIATURE RAILWAY

Manufactured by Meccano Limited, L...

MICKEY MOUSE ANNUAL

LET'S GET TOGETHER AGAIN!

PLAYBOX ANNUAL 1937 1937

COLLINS' AIRCRAFT ANNUAL

G-FAAW

COL. LINDBERGH and SIR ALAN COBHAM

CRACKERS ANNUAL

THE BRUIN BOYS' JOLLY RING GAME

SPEAR'S GAMES

THE BRUIN BOYS
Registered Trade Mark of the Proprietors of "The Rainbow"

SCHOOLGIRLS' OWN ANNUAL 1931

BOYS & GIRLS LIBRARY

Collins

PLAY UP, GREYS!

The Japhet AND Happy ANNUAL 1935

We'll go an' ask the chemist for some gargle for your sore throat, Adelaide!!

Horrabin

News Chronicle Publications Dept. London, E.C.4.

Toys, whether traditional or contemporary, tend to reflect the events of an era. The Olympic Games of 1932 were miniaturised into a boxed game covering everything from the 100-yard-sprint to the high jump. Frog aeroplanes were available from 1932 (the Leopard Moth came in 1936); and Dinky Toys, with their cars and lorries, arrived in 1934 and proved popular at prices from 6d to 9d. Hornby Dublo electric-trains were the excitement of 1938; more realistic than their O'guage clockwork or electric counterparts, Hornby described them as 'the perfect table-top railway'. The full set, as above, would have cost 70/-.

Some 'toys' were also for adults; for instance, jigsaws, football pools games, and Monopoly which came from the USA in 1936, heralded as the 'rage of America'.

Every Christmas saw the latest batch of annuals—extensions of comics, or newspaper cartoon strips like Teddy Tail who had appeared in the Daily Mail since 1915, or Rupert Bear from the Daily Express (since 1920). Mickey Mouse and Popeye were favourites throughout the 1930s, and in 1938 Disney's film of Snow White and the Seven Dwarfs captured children's imagination.

1932

RALEIGH
THE ALL-STEEL BICYCLE

£4.15.9

HERCULES
Sports Light

No. 13 (New Series), Vol. 1   June 18, 1932

The PASSING SHOW
2ᴰ

COUNTY
BUS
SERVICE

★Guinea
Presentation
Shakespeare
offered to Every
Reader—see inside

New Series H

THE NEW SUNBEAM
BICYCLES FOR 193

THE CHILTERNS

ORDNANCE SURVEY
TOURIST MAP

NEW FOREST
G R
SCALE 1-INCH TO 1-MILE

Price : Mounted in Sections, 4/6 Net

ENGLAND AND WALES

WANDERING
ON THE
CONTINENT
WITH THE AID OF
YOUTH HOSTELS
1936

VIA HARWICH, GRIMSBY or HULL

BSA CYCLING
Fashion ANNUAL

BSA CYCLING
Fashion ANNUAL

Cycling and hiking

Love of the great outdoors and a
growing awareness that exercise was healthy,
created a new enthusiasm for walking in the country;
ramblers became known as 'hikers'. Access to the
countryside was now much easier: public transport-
railways, buses, motor coaches - was better than
ever before, and many more people owned cars.
Young couples could escape for a day together;
or, if rain set in, could play the game of 'Hiking'
(two examples can be seen on the right).
Cycling was also popular. Bicycles had high
safety standards, and roads were safer for cyclists.
The Youth Hostels Association had been formed in 1930.

For all outdoor occasions

HIKING FOR ALL
By D. FRANCIS MORGAN

HIKES
IN KENT AND SUSSEX
By JOHN ARROWSMITH

THE HIKER & CAMPER

THE ONLY MAGAZINE CAR... OFFICIAL FEDERATION AND CLUB GOSSIP—FU... FACTS AND REAL A...

JULY

CHILTERN STROLLS & RAMBLES
3d

WHERE RAMBLERS MEET.
The Ruc-Sac 2d
Volume I. No. 5.　　NOVEMBER, 1931.

6d
RAMBLES
SERIES No. 1
PRICE 2d
GREEN LINE

1938

YOUTH HOSTELS ASSOCIA...

THE RAMBLER'S HANDBOOK
1938 EDITION
SOUTHERN　FEDERATION

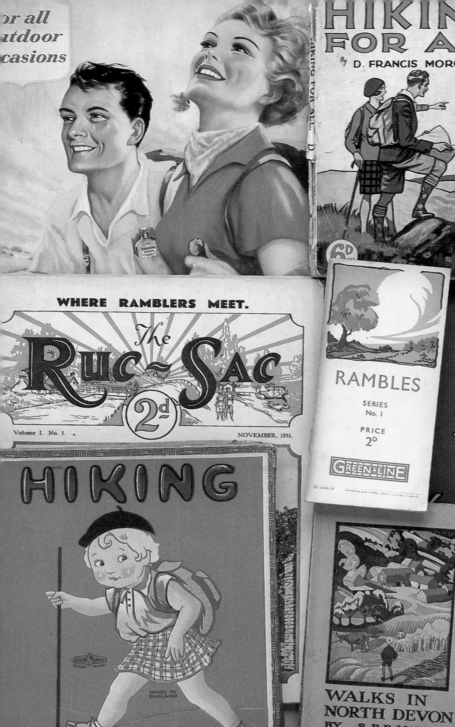
HIKING

WALKS IN NORTH DEVON
BY S.P.B. MAIS
6d
Published by the Southern Railway

CASTLE
OUTINGS
RAIL · TRAM
BUS · COACH

The Radio Times, May 18, 1934
THE RADIO TIMES 2d

HIKING

Radio Times, June 3, 1938　　PRICE TWOPENCE
RADIO TIMES
OPEN-AIR NUMBER
2d

As car ownership grew, so did the accidents.
Thus the 1930s heralded a new awareness of the need for road safety. The Highway Code was first published in 1931 (updated four years later). In 1934 driving tests (which cost 7/6ᵈ) became compulsory for anyone wanting a license; pedestrian crossways were standardised and 'Belisha' beacons introduced (named after the Minister of Transport, Leslie Hore-Belisha), along with a 30mph speed limit in urban areas. At this time there were nearly 1½ million private cars on the road. For road safety, "cat's eyes" were brought into use in 1935. A wide range of cars was on offer, from the powerful Lagonda at £595 to the compact Austin Seven at £120. Car manufacturers advertised their latest models with countryside images and sunlit picnics away from the hurly-burly of modern life and traffic jams. Women were often portrayed at the wheel. Motor cycles, however, were for men with women on the pillion or in the sidecar. A motor cycle could cost from £18 (Wolf 147cc) to £46 (Triumph 2.49 h.p.).

31

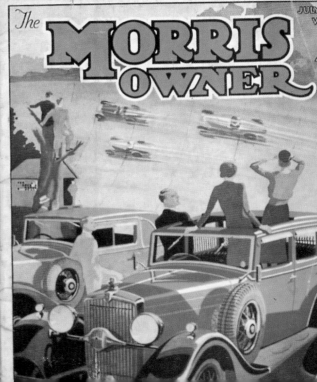

The
1934
HILLMAN MINX

See full description inside

HM 1934

Wolseley's *Crowning Achievement*

THE VERDICT OF OLYMPIA

THE NEW SUPER SIXES

THE NEW
MORRIS
12 H.P. SERIES III

Full description and
road test in this issue

MORRIS
THE CAR WITH THE LOWEST UPKEEP COST

If you don't buy MORRIS – at least buy a car made in the United Kingdom

Sole Exporters: MORRIS INDUSTRIES EXPORTS LTD., COWLEY, OXFORD, ENGLAND

JUNE 1933

The *Austin*
MAGAZINE
AND ADVOCATE
SPECIAL SUMMER NUMBER

4D
VOL. 6
NO. 9

MOTOR·UNION INSURANCE CO LTD.
ALL CLASSES OF INSURANCE TRANSACTED
10, ST. JAMES'S STREET, S.W.1

MORRIS
THE MODERN CAR

21 and 25 h.p. 6 cylinder Saloon from £265
16 and 18 h.p. 6 cylinder Saloon from £250

MORRIS MOTORS

SAFETY **MG** FAST!

THE M.G. 1½ LITRE

Four Door Saloon - £325
Four Seater (Open) - £280
Folding Head Foursome £335
(ex works)

TRIPLEX   DUNLOP
Buy a car made in the United Kingdom

Lincoln-Zephyr

LINCOLN CARS LIMITED
GREAT WEST ROAD
BRENTFORD, MDX.

HUMBER
HUMBER LIMITED
COVENTRY

122

THE CHOICE OF THE EXPERIENCED MOTORIST

"Still the centre
of Interest"— *Austin*
SEVEN

See it on Stand
—also its new broth
"THE BIG SEVEN

The SEVEN Range:—
The Pearl Cabriolet
Ruby Saloon
Ruby Fixed Head Saloon
Open Road Tourer
Two-seater

NEW DE LUXE FORD
(£10 Tax, £7. 10s. in 1935)

£135   **Ford**   £145

Here's a Thrill!

THE NEW
Daimler
2½-LITRE

33

BOOK OF TRAINS
1938-9

HOLIDAY HAUNTS
1939
GWR SIXPENCE

L·N·E·R
HOLIDAY
HANDBOOK
1937
6D

HINTS FOR HOLIDAYS
"The Pull of the South"
Where to go
Where to stay
Over one thousand
Photographs
6D
SOUTHERN RAILWAY

GWR

GLORIOUS
DEVON

N E R

THE TRACK OF THE
CORONATION SCOT

TRAVEL
BY RAIL
with
CIRCULAR TOUR TICKETS
RAILWAYS
BRITISH
CIRCULAR TOUR
TICKET
ANYWHERE
TO
ANYWHERE
IN GREAT BRITAIN
FARE £
ISSUED ON
for
BUSINESS
or
PLEASURE
TOURS
ALL THE
YEAR ROUND

THE PEERLESS RIVIERA
including—
ROME · CORSICA · MALTA & BRIONI ISLANDS
SOUTHERN RAILWAY
6D

HOLIDAY
1937
HAUNT
CORONATION EDITION
SIXP
GW

IGHT TRAVEL
TICKETS
T HALF FARES
NORTH OF ENGLAND
JULY to 26th SEPTEMBER 1937

FACTS ABOUT
BRITISH
RAILWAYS

SUMMER
1935

SUMMER 1934
OUTINGS &
EXCURSIONS
LONDON TRANSPORT

SCARBOROUGH
FLIER
No 2747

EASTER 1930
1932
BY
LONDON'S

IN & AROUND
LONDON
BY
LONDONS UNDERGROUND
SUMMER 1932

Seeing
GLASGOW
BY TRAM
AND BUS
1938

The would-be holiday maker
to a British resort found ample information
from which to decide on a destination.
The preferred way to travel was by rail,
now offering economic fares (often at
a 1d a mile). A week's stay at a hotel
or boarding house cost from 2 to 6
guineas depending on the season, August
being the most expensive. Seaside resorts
vied with each other to offer best-record
sunshine and golden sands, golf and
tennis facilities, entertainment and
piers. Where Newquay had surf
riding, Blackpool had its Tower,
ballrooms and Opera House.

35

GASTRONOMIC HUNGARY

SEEING CHICAGO THE GRAY LINE

TRAVELERS HOTEL GUIDE
WINTER AND SPRING EDITION 1931
Compliments of
WHITE STAR LINE

DOLOMITES
MERANO
VENICE-LIDO
GARDONE LAKE GARDA

TOURS IN THE SOVIET

TOKYO SIGHTSEEING

THE GRAY LINE

NICE 1933
CARNAVAL
PROGRAMME DES FÊTES

DENMARK

ENGLAND

For tickets and all information apply to:
THE DANISH TOURIST BUREAU, Ltd.
31, Haymarket, London. S. W. 1.

KURORT MILLSTATT AM SEE
KÄRNTEN·ÖSTERREICH·AUSTRIA

IN AMERICA
TRAVEL EVERYWHERE BY
GREYHOUND Lines

49, LEADENHALL STREET, LONDON, E.C.2.
A. B. REYNOLDSON, General European Agent.

OF PROGRESS POSITION-1934

SEE CHICAGO

THE TOKYO MOTOR BUS CO., LTD.
TEL.—SHITAYA. 8141, 8142

CHICAGO SURFACE LINES

BRASIL
CALENDARIO TURISTICO
DO DISTRICTO FEDERAL
CIDADE DO RIO DE JANEIRO

1937

JAPAN

Burgenstock
Schweiz

What to see in AUSTRIA
PRINTED IN AUSTRIA

Travel Germany

AUSTRALIA CALLS YOU

CAIRO

MONTE CARLO

SOVIET ARMENIA

My Trip Through the Panama Canal
From the
ATLANTIC to the PACIFIC

A SCENIC WONDERLAND OF MILD WINTER... AND GLORIOUS SUMMER

Ease of travel and its relative cheapness enabled the middle classes to have their 'Grand Tour' round Europe, enticed by colourful brochures that offered sun, snow or Continental cuisine. More distant places could also be offered – Russia, Japan, Cairo, Australia and the sights of the Chicago World's fair of 1933

Everyone dreamt of a holiday voyage on a sea-going liner, and increasingly during the 1930s more people could afford one. The high life aboard ship was seen as the ultimate luxury — basking in the sun, seeing the world, playing deck quoits or shuffle board. For £20 a return trip to Teneriffe could be booked, or to America for £38 return.

Flying always gained much public attention. For flying enthusiasts there were magazines - the more adventurous could build their own "Flea" for about £150. In the 1930s commercial air travel could reach most parts of the world. In 1933 the morning flight left Croydon Airport at 9 a.m., arrived at Le Bouget, Paris, at 11.15 a.m., and cost £8-11-0 return. Along with the passengers went the airmail. Jigsaws and cigarette cards (1938) celebrate the Empire Flying Boat.

MAE WEST and CARY GRANT

WIN A CAR FOR 1/- OVER 200

FLICKERS
1/-

FILM WEEKLY, Saturday, September 17, 1938.   Registered at the G.P.O. as a Newspaper

The National Guide to Films
Film Weekly
3D
SATURDAY
SEPTEMBER 17
1938

The Smart Screen Magazine
SCREENLAND
June
NOW 15c
30c in Canada

Greta
Garbo

TUREGOER
2d
WEEKLY

£7,500
FREE
FILM CONTEST

Eugene O'Ne...
Daring Dram...
"STRANGE I...
with Norma ...
and Clark ...
fictionized fro...

The PICTUREGOER
SUMMER
ANNUAL
6D

NORMA
SHEARER

LILIAN HARVEY: by LESLIE BANKS
Film Pictorial
Film Pictorial, Vol. V. No. 208.   Registered at the G.P.O. as a newspaper
MARCH 17, 1934
2D
Weekly

Katharine Hepburn and
Douglas Fairbanks Jnr.

Andy Hardy
meets Debutante
with

LEWIS STONE
MICKEY ROONEY
CECILIA PARKER
FAY HOLDEN
ANN RUTHERFORD
DIANA LEWIS
JUDY
GAR...

No. 2495

FRANCIS, DAY & HUNTER LTD.
138-140, Charing Cross Road, W.C.2

YOU...
Words b...

Metro-Goldwyn-Mayer's
GIANT ENTERTAINMENT
BROADWAY MELODY
of 1936

Repertoire
YOU ARE MY LUCKY STAR
ON A SUNDAY AFTERNOON
I'VE GOT A FEELIN'
YOU'RE FOOLIN'
SING BEFORE BREAKFAST
BROADWAY RHYTHM
Price 6d Each Copy

featuring ROBERT TAYLOR
ELEANOR POWELL

6D

JEAN HARLOW Tells What Hollywood Has Taught Her
MOTION PICTURE
JUNE
NOW 10c
In Canada 11c

MARLENE
DIETRICH

DON'T TALK
TO ME ABOUT LOVE
...SAYS WILLIAM POWELL

Cinemas had become regal palaces with
imposing art deco facades and interiors
as glamourous as the Busby Berkley
routines they screened. It was the film stars
who made the news, promoted by the studios:
film magazines, both British and American
were the chief means of promotion. However,
in films using special effects like 'King Kong'
(1933) and in cartoon films like Walt Disney's
Snow White (1938), cinematic technology was
itself the star. It could be said that in some
spectacular effects for 'Gone with the Wind'
(1939), the performances of Clark Gable and
Vivien Leigh were upstaged.

43

By 1930, the radio had become the gathering point for the family — to listen to music, the latest sporting event, the news, Children's Hour, or a favourite comedy show. Most homes had a radio: Ekco, Philips, Ferguson, HMV, Vidor, Murphy and Cossor all had radios within the popular price range of £5 to £15. By the end of 1932 five million radio licences were sold at 10/- (a dog licence cost 7/6d a year).

The Radio Times at 2d a week was the key to programme details and achieved a weekly sale of up to 3 million copies. Well-known artists were employed to illustrate the Summer, Christmas and Holiday issues — H M Bateman, Stanley Herbert, Bob Sherriffs, Eric Fraser and S C Johnson. More often, the Radio Times just had black and white covers.

WELDON'S HOME DRESSMAKER

DANCE FROCKS

4d No. 439

FREE! Patterns of ALL these Last Word Styles

LAMBETH WALK

No. 2474

BOOMPS-A-DAISY!

A NEW OLD-FASHIONED PARTY DANCE.

IN THE MOOD

THE "JITTERBUG" CRAZE.

THE CHESTNUT TREE

'neath the Spreading Chestnut Tree
The Novelty Singing Dance Sensation

SONG FOX-TROT
Words by AL DUBIN
Music by HARRY WARREN

Featured by AMBROSE AND HIS EMBASSY CLUB ORCHESTRA

GOLDERS GREEN HIPPODROME

No. 2218

WELDON'S
Children's Fancy Dress 6d

The Palais Glide

No. 2618

Introducing—
LITTLE BROWN JUG
and WAITING AT THE CHURCH
by HARRIS WESTON

with description by D.T. FOSTER B.A.T.D.

SAVOY THEATRE

WONDER BAR

BY ARRANGEMENT WITH C. EGERTON KILLICK &

(NEW
Written
REN S

FEATURE
by

FRANCIS

WINDOW BILL

JUST WHAT EVERYBODY WANTS!

Columbia PORTABLES—

CARRIES 8 RECORDS IN THE LID

MODEL 202
IN BLUE, RED OR BLACK
THE "DE LUXE" OF

MODEL 204
WITH CARRIER FOR FOURTEEN RECORDS
THE FAVOURITE

MODEL 205
52/6
THE BIGGEST SELLER IN

"O-KAY FOR SOUND"

A GEORGE BLACK Production

LONDON PALLADIUM

6d

Cheerio

FEATURED by MAX MILLER in

BY W.H. KITCHEN AND J. WESTGARTH
ADDITIONAL LYRICS BY MICHAEL CARR

GEORGE BLACK's NEW SHOW
APPLE SAUCE

2ND PRIZE WINNING SONG IN THE NEWS CHRONICLE SONG COMPETITION

PRICE 1/-

INTERIOR OF THE GRAND THEATRE

Radiating Pleasure to the World

SOUVENIR PROGRAMME

TOWER & WINTER GARDENS
BLACKPOOL

REVUDEVILLE

SOUVENIR of Nos. 41 to 50

THIRD EDITION

WINDMILL
PICCADILLY CIRCUS

1/-

The 'big band' so
pervaded homes
Thirties were f
dances like th
the energetic Jitt
Miller and the
was all the rag-

Then there was t
service was sta
the high defini
number of view
broadcast in 1
at the outbreak
television sets
great possibili
predicted that

46

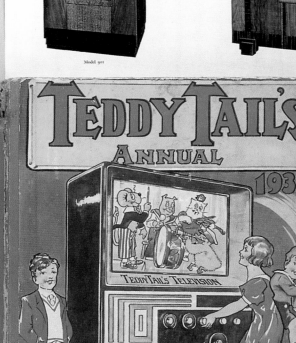

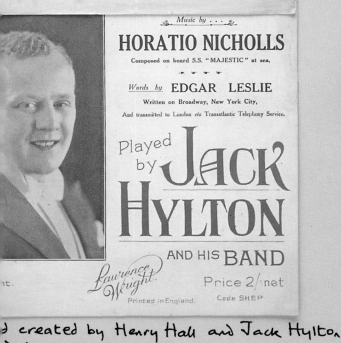

...d created by Henry Hall and Jack Hylton
...o dance halls, which by the end of the
... of couples experimenting with novelty
...ambeth Walk and Palais Glide, and in 1939
...ng craze from America. Comedians like Max
...azy Gang appeared in vaudeville. Fancy dress
...at parties.
...vision, the novelty of the age. A regular
...d by The BBC in 1932, but it was not until
...n service began in 1936 that the small
...began to increase. Wimbledon was first
... By the time transmissions were suspended
...of war in September 1939, around 20,000
...re in use (in the South of England). Some foresaw
...s for television: The Modern Boy comic of 1937
...e future presents would be chosen by viewing Tv.

In the early 1930s a coupon war was raging between cigarette companies, but by mutual agreement this ended in 1933. Cigarette cards were still issued up to the war; some series had their own booklets like Speedway Riders (the second biggest spectator sport). Consulate was launched in 1932 with a deco pack, as Du Maurier had been since 1929.

50

POST OFFICE TELEGRAPHS.

NIGHT TELEGRAPH LETTERS

NIGHT TELEGRAPH LETTERS

INLAND TELEGRAMS

TELEGRAM

DELIVERING A TELEGRAM

**DON'T·BE·OFFENDED
IT'S
VALENTINE
DAY**

You wear your diamonds and your pearls
In such a swanky manner,
But we know you get them all, old girl,
At Woolworth's for a tanner!

**TO REMIND YOU
BATCH
TELEGRAMS
A NEW TELEGRAPH FACILITY
FOR BUSINESS MEN**

**IS·ONLY·A·VALENTINE
JOKE·FOR
VALENTINE
DAY**

You swank about your City job
(Ten hours a day for thirty bob)
T'would be better than spending it all on
your back,
If you h

HOW TO ADDRESS

LETTERS AND PARCELS

**POST
YOUR PARCELS**

TELEPHONE

The Telephone in the Home

You need never lack companionship when the telephone is in your home.

You wonder if the Browns can come to supper. Telephone them. You want a chat with some friend, now. Telephone her. You have forgotten some provisions. Telephone for them. The confectioner has sent the wrong cakes. Telephone him. You want another hand for Bridge. Telephone.

Why has your boy not come home from school? Telephone.

When does the "big" picture start in the cinema. Telephone. You want seats in the theatre. Telephone for them.

Your children are away at school. Keep in touch by telephone.

Birthdays, weddings, anniversaries. Send greetings by telephone.

You are anxious about something? Telephone.

You don't feel like shopping to-day? Telephone your orders.

DON'T WAIT—TELEPHONE.

**HOLD
THE LINE**

**RAILEX
SERVICE**

**CONSIDER YOUR
COLOUR SCHEME**

**COME ON!
THE TELEPHONE**

*I haven't a waist any more -
it's a circumference*

As the telephone had reached many people's homes, and the cost had been reduced to 1d - 4d for local calls, its popularity was increasing rapidly. Easy to use, and instant, the telephone was fast replacing the postcard (1d postage), the letter (1½d postage) and the telegram (6 words for 6d). The saucy seaside postcard, however, still prospered.

With telegrams being used much less, the Post Office eventually started a Greetings Telegram service on 24th July 1935 (many other countries had by this time started their own). Each of these special telegram forms was designed by an established artist such as Rex Whistler and Frank Newbold. In 1936 Valentine Telegrams were introduced. Greetings telegrams proved to be much in demand at 9d for 9 words (1d for each additional word) and in 1938 over four million were sent.

*I've met a grass widow down here
So I am going to be a vegetarian*

*"Do you think you can manage 'er alone, sir,
or do you want any help?"*

Pain, Standard, Wilder, Wells and Brock were all well-established fireworks manufacturers providing bangers and crash for Guy Fawkes Day each year, or the hugely popular indoor fireworks for the more genteel. Apart from the traditional sparklers, rockets and Roman candles, more topical names included Traffic Signal, Boy Scout and Halley's Comet (last seen in 1910).

Mead & Field's
MARIONETTE Crackers
MANUFACTURED BY MEAD & FIELD LTD. IN LONDON ENGLAND.

Batger's
Animal Luggage Crackers
PRINTED
ENG

XMAS TIME
Crackers
Cecil Coleman Ltd.

Batger's
Forfeit
Crackers
PRINTED IN ENGLAND

BATGERS
"HARLEQUIN"
REGD TRADE MARK
CRACKERS

Batger's
FORTUNE TELLING Crackers
THE NAME GUARANTEE OF VALUE

Barratt's
XMAS
FUN
MADE IN ENGLAND.
CRAC

In 1937 a box of Holiday Crackers (top right) would cost 28/-, and 36/- for fort
crackers (bottom left). Unusually, the musical gifts were stuck to the outside of

TOYLAND CRACKERS

BATGER'S "HARLEQUIN" CRACKERS

BATGER'S XMAS

XMAS CRAC

HOLIDAYS CRACKERS

THE NAME BATGER IS A GUARANTEE OF VALUE

"The Geisha" CRACKERS

Cecil Coleman Ltd

Midget Christmas Crackers

Containing CHARMS & JEWELS

THE "BRUIN BOYS" CRACKERS.

WE SHOULD LIKE A CRACKER MRS BRUIN.

COPYRIGHT BY ARRANGEMENT WITH THE PROPRIETORS OF THE RAINBOW

XMAS EXPRESS

CRACKER EXPRESS

CRACKER

PRINTED IN ENGLAND

MUSICAL TOY

Crackers

TOM SMITH'S CAPS

TOM SMITH'S HATS & CAPS CRACKERS.

615

KERS

Teller ch cracker.

55

GOD SAVE OUR KING

KING EDWARD VIII

"MAY HEAVEN'S CHOICEST BLESSINGS,
THAT CAN COME FROM GOD ALONE
BE SHOWERED FROM THE SKY ABOVE
UPON HIM AND HIS ROYAL THRONE."

WEEKLY ILLUSTRATED 2ᴰ
Saturday, February 1, 1936. No. 31. VOL. II

H.M.
EDWARD VIII
ALLY ENLARGED
ENIR NUMBER

TUCK'S CORONATION crêpe
10 FEET LONG
WATERFAST
20 INCHES WIDE
COLOURS
RAPHAEL TUCK & SONS . LT
RAPHAEL HOUSE MOORFIELDS .E.C.2.
MADE IN ENGLAND

KING EDWARD CHOCOLATES

SUPREME FOR FOUR REIGNS
1936
Burdall's

On 6ᵗʰ May 1935
King George V and
Queen Mary celebrated
their Silver Jubilee. In
every corner of Britain Street
parties were held. Every kind
of manufacturer leaped at the
opportunity to produce souvenirs.
Chocolate bars, egg cups, mugs and
magazines all commemorated the
happy occasion. George V died in
January 1936. Edward VIII became King,
but the souvenirs (on this page) were
for a coronation that never happened—
Edward VIII abdicated
before the event (due on
12ᵗʰ May 1937)

CORONATION 1937

KING EDWARD
DIEU ET MON DROIT

CORONATION KING EDWARD

The Coronation of George VI and Queen Elizabeth took place on 12th May 1937, and once again Britain was festooned with souvenirs, which were kept carefully in families as keepsakes of the big event. Manufacturers produced tablets of soap embossed with the profiles of their majesties. Processions in boxes (see the two examples above) were available, when the whole retinue of soldiers, bandsmen, carriages and royal coach could be 'wheeled through' by turning a handle. The Coronation Puzzle could be solved by guiding a silver ball around the pitfalls of the processional route (a steady hand required). But the most intricate souvenir was the nutshell that contained sixteen photographs of the royal family, including the popular Princesses, Elizabeth and Margaret.

SUNDAY PICTORIAL
ARTICLE BY THE LATE SIR SEFTON BRANCKER
R101 FUNERAL MEMORIAL NUMBER
SALE VASTLY IN EXCESS OF ANY OTHER PICTURE PAPER IN THE WORLD
No. 913 SUNDAY, OCTOBER 12, 1930 Twopence
FOR THEY REST FROM THEIR LABOURS

DAILY SKETCH
WOMAN OUGHT TO PAY, by CANDIDUS
RODDIE OR DUMPY?—PAGE 25
FRIDAY, MAY 17, 1935 ONE PENNY
1s. 6d.-AN-HOUR AEROPLANE
London to Paris at Cost of 6/-

DAILY SKETCH
WHEN WOMEN STORMED PARLIAMENT: Page 7
AT THE CINEMA: by D'ALROY
THURSDAY, JULY 4, 1935 ONE PENNY
PERRY BEATS HIS OLD RIVAL
HE WILL DEFEND HIS TITLE IN ANGLO-GERMAN FINAL

DAILY SKETCH
MR. SNOWDEN'S PROTEST: THE PLAIN TRUTH (Page 4)
EVELYN LAYE TO-DAY
SATURDAY, FEBRUARY 14, 1931 ONE PENNY
CAPT. MALCOLM CAMPBELL'S SPEED TRIUMPH: FIRST PICTURES

DAILY SKETCH
BACK TO TWO PARTY POLITICS: By CANDIDUS
SECOND DAY ELECTION RESULTS
SATURDAY, NOVEMBER 16, 1935 ONE PENNY
GOVERNMENT'S BIG MARGIN
Majority of 246 With Only Few Results To Come

STATE OF THE PARTIES

THE DAILY MAIL
Weather Outlook : Fair; Slight Showers
Broadcasting : Page 9
LAST ISSUE
HULL FACILITIES FOR HIGHER EDUCATION —PAGE TEN
CERTIFIED NET SALE EXCEEDS 81,000 COPIES PER DAY
No. 15,556. HULL, TUESDAY, SEPTEMBER 3, 1935. One Penny
SIR MALCOLM CAMPBELL'S AMAZING NEW SPEED RECORD
304·311 m.p.h.
Over Five Miles a Minute in British Bluebird
TYRE BURSTS AFTER FIRST RUN, BUT DRIVER UNPERTURBED
British Mandate Over Abyssinia?
"BEST WAY OUT OF DESPERATE SITUATION"
New Suggestion in Addis Ababa

The People
FREE HAIR BEAUTY COUPON
NICHOLSON'S GIN IN EVERY COCKTAIL
SUNDAY, JANUARY 26, 1936
No. 2836 55th Year OVER 3,000,000 CERTIFIED SALE 2D.
HOW THE WORLD WILL MOURN
On Tuesday a Common Sympathy will Bring All Races Together
NATIONS OF SILENT SORROW
250,000 PILGRIMS IN THE RAIN
COLOUR · FILM £4,000,000 RACE WON BY BRITAIN

Evening Standard
CLOSING CITY PRICES
FINAL NIGHT
Hoyo DE MONTERREY HAVANA CIGARS
No. 33,936 LONDON, THURSDAY, DECEMBER 10, 1936 ONE PENNY
THE KING ABDICATES
Duke of York Monarch

Sunday Graphic
and SUNDAY NEWS
MY OFFER TO THE WORLD, By HITLER: SEE P. 12
SECRET AGENT P 33 CONFESSES
No. 1,092 SUNDAY, MARCH 8, 1936 TWOPENCE
HITLER OCCUPIES RHINE
Locarno Denounced — Troops March
BIG GUNS ENTER COLOGNE

Daily Mirror
ONE PENNY
DUKE OF YORK IS OUR NEW KING

DAILY SKETCH
MILLIONS SEE GREAT FIRE
PALACE BLAZE: PAGES OF PICTURES
TUESDAY, DECEMBER 1, 1936 ONE PENNY
CENTURY'S BIGGEST FIRE RAZES CRYSTAL PALACE
Crowds Leap Screaming to Safety From Path of Molten Glass
DUKE OF KENT SEES BLAZE

Daily Express
WORLD'S LARGEST DAILY SALE
MODEL GLIDER
Friday, September 30, 1938
The Daily Express declares that Britain will not be involved in a European war this year, or next year
PEACE
Agreement last night in Munich
GERMAN TROOPS IN THE "UNIFORM"

Sunday Graphic
MUSSOLINI: DRAMATIC PEACE MOVE
Have a CAPSTAN
LATE LONDON EDITION
No. 1,274 SUNDAY, SEPTEMBER 3, 1939 TWOPENCE
Premier's 'Definite Statement To-day'
CABINET MEETS AT MIDNIGHT
THERE WAS A SURPRISE MEETING OF THE CABINET JUST BEFORE MIDNIGHT. IT LASTED FIFTY MINUTES.

EVENTS OF THE 1930s

1930 Amy Johnson's solo flight to Australia. R101 airship crashed killing 44 people. Youth Hostel Association founded. Arthur Ransome's book 'Swallows and Amazons'. Oxydol soap powder launched.

1931 Ramsey MacDonald became Prime Minister of National Government to sort out economic crisis. Malcolm Campbell broke land speed record in Blue Bird car reaching 245 mph. Highway Code published. Unemployment at 2·7 million: population 44.8m

1932 Sir Oswald Mosley formed British Union of fascists. Aldous Huxley's book 'Brave New World'. Olympic Games held in Los Angeles. Aga cookers now built in Britain. First Christmas broadcast by George V. Woman's Own magazine. Launch of Twiglets, Weetabix, Mars bars, Dettol.

1933 Adolf Hitler Chancellor of Germany. Campbell speeds up to 272 mph. Henry Beck designed new Underground map. King Kong film. Anglepoise lamp designed by George Carwardine. Black Magic chocs.

1934 Fred Perry won Wimbledon (and in 1935 and '36). Telephone kiosk designed by Sir Giles Gilbert Scott. National electricity grid completed. Driving tests compulsory. Donald Duck film. Belisha beacon pedestrian crossing. Dinky Toys (in 1933 called Meccano Miniatures)

1935 Stanley Baldwin became Tory Prime Minister. George V and Queen Mary's Silver Jubilee. Greetings Telegram service begun. Hitchcock's film 'The Thirty-Nine Steps'. Campbell broke 300 mph speed barrier. Cat's eyes road markings. Aluminium milk bottle tops. Penguin paperback books. Ovaltineys, beer cans, Aero, Quality Street.

1936 Crystal Palace destroyed by fire. George V died. Abdication of Edward VIII. Spanish Civil War (till 1939). BBC Television service started. Jarrow crusade march to London. Olympic Games in Berlin. Maiden voyage of Cunard's Queen Mary (launched 1934). Monopoly.

1937 Coronation of George VI. Neville Chamberlain Prime Minister. George Orwell's book 'The Road to Wigan Pier'. Billy Butlin opened holiday camp at Skegness. 'Woman' magazine. Dandy comic. Smarties, Rolos, Nestlé's Milky Bar, Kit Kat (in 1935 called Chocolate Crisp).

1938 Empire Exhibition opens in Glasgow. Queen Elizabeth launched. Disney's film 'Snow White'. Picture Post magazine. Beano comic. Cadbury's Roses chocolates.

1939 'Gone With The Wind' and 'Wizard of Oz' films. Germany invades Poland — war declared. National Identity cards. Jitterbug dance. Nescafé instant coffee.